Dedicated To:
Sasha Herron & Family
A strong woman and motherly figure

Written By: Abigail Gartland

Hello, my name is St. Mary Magdalene!

I was born in the very 1st century in Magdala.

When I was younger,
I struggled in my life.

I was very far away from God, and was taken over by sadness

One day, I was overcome by my sadness, when I met a man named, Jesus.

Jesus told me that he loved me, and took away all my sadness.

I was so grateful, and decided to follow Jesus for the rest of my life.

I spent all my days with Jesus, up until He died on the cross for us.

When Jesus died, I was the most sad that I have ever been.

Every day after He died, I visited Jesus' tomb.

On the third day, I went to his tomb to visit, but there was something very wrong.

I became very scared, but then saw a man who I thought was the gardener.

He was in all white, and I realized it was actually Jesus!

I ran to find the other disciples to tell them the good news.

I have always been a loyal follower of Jesus.

Do you want to be more like me?

You can celebrate my feast day with me on July 22nd.

I am the patron saint of converts!

I pray for you every day of your life.

St. Mary Magdalene, Pray for Us

Copyright:

Clipart:
Licensed purchased: 1/10/2024

About the Author

Abigail Gartland

I love the saints and I love my faith. The idea for sharing the stories of the saints with little ones came when my dear friends were expecting their first baby. I wanted to create something as unique and special as our friendship. Each book is dedicated to very special people and groups who have enriched my faith in different ways. I am blessed to write these stories and appreciate the unending support of my family and friends. When I am not writing, I'm a middle school teacher. I hope you enjoy these stories. I pray for each and every person who opens one of my books to learn more about the saints.

Abbie

www.ingramcontent.com/pod-product-compliance
Lightning Source LLC
LaVergne TN
LVHW051042070526
838201LV00067B/4890